WHAT AM I?

Bouncy, Big, and Furry

WHAT AM I?

By Moira Butterfield
Illustrated by Wayne Ford

RSVP

RAINTREE
STECK-VAUGHN
PUBLISHERS
The Steck-Vaughn Company

Austin, Texas

Published by Raintree Steck-Vaughn Publishers, an imprint of Steck-Vaughn Company.

Editors: Stephanie Bellwood, Heather Luff
Project Manager: Joyce Spicer
Designer: Helen James
Illustrator: Wayne Ford / Wildlife Art Agency
Consultant: Andrew Branson

Library of Congress Cataloging-in-Publication Data

Butterfield, Moira, 1961-
    Bouncy, big, and furry / by Moira Butterfield; illustrated by Wayne Ford.
        p.   cm. — (What am I?)
    Summary: A riddle asking the reader to guess which animal is being described precedes information about different parts of a red kangaroo's body, how it behaves, and where it lives.
    ISBN 0-8172-4589-8 (hardcover)
    ISBN 0-8172-7228-3 (softcover)
    1. Red kangaroo — Juvenile literature. [1. Red kangaroo. 2. Kangaroos.] I. Ford, Wayne, ill. II. Title. III. Series.
QL737.M35B875   1998
599.2'223 — dc21
                      97-5404
                      CIP   AC

Printed in Hong Kong
Bound in the United States.
1 2 3 4 5 6 7 8 9 0 WO 01 00 99 98 97

My feet are big.
My tail is long.
I do not walk, I bound along.
I have a pouch
that is soft and warm
to keep my baby safe from harm.

What am I?

Here is my foot.

My feet help me
to bound along as
fast as a moving car.
I hop a long way
when I jump.

This wild dingo
might attack me.
If it comes too close,
I will kick it hard
with my feet.

Here is my tail.

It is long and strong.
I lean back on it to
rest. I hit other
animals with it
when I fight.

When I hop, my tail
sticks out behind
me. It helps me
keep my balance
as I jump.

Here are my arms.

I have sharp claws.
I use them to
comb my fur and
to hurt my enemies
in a fight.

Sometimes I lick
my wrists with
my long tongue.
It cools me down
when I feel hot.

Here is my fur.

I am female, so my fur is gray. Males have red fur. Can you see a female and a male?

The sun is very hot where I live. I lie in the shade of a tree or in the long grass.

Here is my pouch.

It looks like a
pocket on the
front of my belly.
Do you think
it is empty?

Only females, like
me, have a pouch.
Inside it is warm
and cozy. Can you
guess what my
pouch is for?

Here is my eye.

I look for tasty plants
to eat. My favorite
food is the chewy
grass that grows
where I live.

I live with other animals
like me. I can see
two males fighting.
The strongest
one will win.

Here are my ears.

I can hear things that are far away.
If I hear something that frightens me,
I warn my friends of danger.

I beat my tail on the ground...
thump, thump, thump!
Have you guessed what I am?

I am a kangaroo.

Point to my...

sharp claws.

strong legs.

short arms.

pointed ears.

big feet.

long tail.

I am called a
red kangaroo.
I am female, and
my fur is gray.

Here is my baby.

It is called a joey.
When a joey is born,
it is tiny. It stays in
my pouch until it
grows bigger.

Soon the joey can
hop in and out
of my pouch.
Sometimes its legs
and tail stick out
of the pouch.

23

Here is my home.

I live on the grassland.
How many kangaroos can you see?

Can you see three dingoes, two lizards, two birds called kookaburras, and a flying animal called a sugar glider?

Here is a map of the world.

I live in the
country of
Australia where
it is very hot.
Can you find it
on the map?

Can you point to the
place where you live?

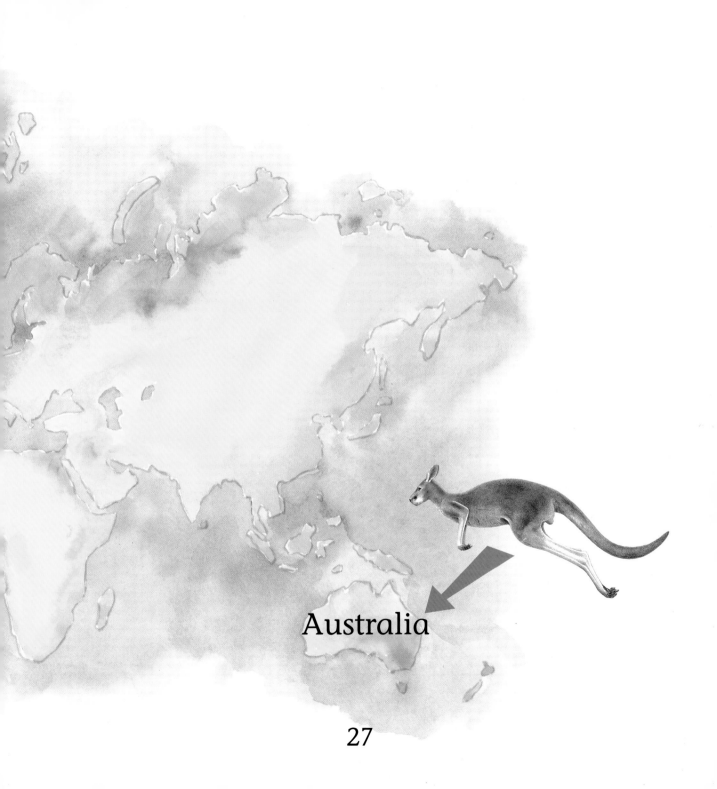

Australia

Can you answer these questions about me?

What do I use my tail for?

What color is the fur of a male kangaroo?

How do I keep cool?

What do I like to eat?

What is my
baby called?

What do I use my
claws for?

Where do I live?

Where does my baby
stay safe and warm?

Here are words to help you learn about me.

bound The way I jump with both feet in the air.

claws My long, sharp nails. I use them to comb my fur and scratch my enemies.

dingo A wild dog found in Australia.

female An animal that can have babies. Girls and women are female.

grassland A dry, grassy place.

joey The name for a baby kangaroo.

male An animal that cannot have babies. Boys and men are male.

pouch A pocket in the belly of female kangaroos. A baby grows inside the pouch.

shade A shadowy place where it is cool. I like to lie in the shade.

wrists The place where my front paws join my arms.